LEVELS OF LIQUIDITY

THE NET WORTH BIBLE WORKBOOK

Know what you have. Know what it's for.
Know when — and when never — to touch it.

STEVEN E. LABROI

Based on the work of

Financial Erudition of African Americans
Build Your Human Equity Line of Credit

Assets − Liabilities = Net Worth

Copyright & Disclaimer

LEVELS OF LIQUIDITY: The Net Worth Bible Workbook

ISBN: 979-8-9962706-0-6
Library of Congress Control Number
LCCN: 2026913688
www.labroiinsurancegroup.com
www.stevenlabroi.com
www.levelsofliquidity.com

The information contained in this book is provided for educational and informational purposes only and is not intended as legal, tax, investment, or financial advice. The strategies, examples, and concepts discussed reflect the author's experience, research, and professional perspective, but financial decisions should always be made in consultation with qualified professionals.

Neither the author nor any affiliated organizations make any representations or warranties with respect to the accuracy, completeness, or applicability of the content to any individual's specific circumstances. Past performance is not indicative of future results. All investing and financial strategies carry risk.

The reader assumes full responsibility for any actions taken based on the information provided in this book.

> Someone has to be the first. Make sure someone is also the last to start from nothing.

Steven E. LaBroi

Steven E. LaBroi

For every family that ever sat on a bare chair
and believed a cushion was coming.
This one is for you.

To the matriarchs of my family —
the women who held everything together
before there was a framework for it.

Great-Grandmothers

Gussie McCullom · Alma Williams

Grandmothers

Ethel Coffey · Rosella LaBroi

Mother

Mary L. LaBroi

TABLE OF CONTENTS

LEVELS OF LIQUIDITY
The Net Worth Bible Workbook

Epigraph

Dedication

Foreword

Who This Workbook Is For

How to Use This Workbook

Quick Start – Build One Cushion Today

Levels Map – The Chair & Cushions

Progress Tracker – My Next 90 Days

Section Zero: The Human Equity Line of Credit 1

Section One: The Chair 10

Couple Script – 12-Minute Money Peace Check-In 12

Section Two: What Is a Level of Liquidity? 13

Couple Script – The "Before We Spend" Pause 17

Section Three: The Tax Illusion 19

Section Four: My Asset Inventory 24

Section Five: My Build Plan 33

TABLE OF CONTENTS

Section Six: My Liquidation Conditions 36

Section Seven: My Economy Playbook 45

Community Check-In 47

Section Eight: The Next Generation Commitment 48

Section Nine: My Level 6 Vision – 100 Years Forward 54

Section Ten: Building Your Private Family Office 66

Filled Examples – How a Completed Page Looks 76

Case Studies 79

Case Study Overview 81

- Marcus 83
- Danielle 88
- Jordan and Maya 93
- The Thompsons 98
- Renee 103

Liquidity Basics – What This Is All About 108

Glossary of Key Terms 110

Affirmations 113

Notes 115

About the Author 117

Connect with the Author 119

Foreword

There is a conversation that happens around kitchen tables, in living rooms, during family reunions, and family Zoom meetings across generations in communities all over the world that never makes it into financial textbooks.

It is not a conversation about real estate, index funds, or diversifying portfolios. It is a quieter conversation — the one where someone lowers their voice and says: How do we stop losing what we build? How do we make sure what I worked for does not disappear the moment I am gone? How do we stop starting over? How do we get this financial foundation started?

That conversation has been happening for generations. However, now more than ever, with the amount of information flowing across the World Wide Web and even Artificial Intelligence. What has truly been missing is a framework and blueprint — a language and map precise enough to answer it, accessible enough to teach it, and honest enough to start where people actually start. Not where some guru thinks you should start

The work you are holding in your hands is that framework and blueprint.

Levels of Liquidity does something no financial education program built for first-generation wealth builders has done before. It does not begin with assumptions about what you already have in place.

It begins with the chair — the hard, splintered, nail-studded starting point that most of us know intimately and that most financial books pretend does not exist. So, from that chair - YOUR CHAIR, it builds a complete, original, actionable architecture for wealth that spans not one lifetime, but generations to come.

You don't have to understand every financial term today. You don't have to have every cushion already. You just have to begin with truth: the chair is real—and so is the future you're building.

Start small. Keep your commitments. Come back to this workbook regularly. The people who inherit your name will not remember every sacrifice you made—
but they will live inside the structure your consistency created.
The chair is real.
So are the cushions.
Let's build.
— On behalf of every family that deserves a framework built for them

The concepts in this workbook — the dual-level principle, the self-liquidating asset category, the Tax Illusion, the Build Principle, the reinvestment routing rule, and the Level 6 generational vision — are not borrowed from existing frameworks. They were developed specifically for first-generation builders, for families who are not continuing wealth but creating it.

This is not a book about getting rich. It is a book about building something that outlasts you. That distinction matters more than any investment strategy ever could.

The student who completes this workbook will do something most Americans — regardless of income — have never done. They will assign every asset a purpose, write a plan to build it, commit in writing to when it can and cannot be touched, and declare what they are building for future generations who will carry their name one hundred years from now.

That is not a financial exercise. That is a transformation.

Read carefully. But more importantly—write. This workbook is not built for perfect people. It is built for committed people. The kind of people who decide, in calm and stressful moments, what their money is for—so fear doesn't take over and decide later.

If you're doing this alone, you can still build. If you're doing this with a spouse, a parent, a sibling, or a trusted friend—pause often and do the pages together.

Wealth that lasts is rarely built in isolation. It is built in households and reinforced in the community.

This can be the new nation-building exercise. Groups, organizations, churches, and neighborhood groups.

Who This Workbook Is For

Most financial books assume you already have a blueprint.
This workbook is for the families building one.

This workbook is for:

- Couples, singles, and families building wealth for the first time (no inheritance, no roadmap)
- People who are tired of starting over every generation
- Builders who want a warm, values-forward system that holds up under pressure
- Anyone ready to stop making money decisions in crisis and start making them in writing
- Working career professionals who, although are experts in their field, need a tru

This workbook is NOT for:

- People looking for a "get rich quick" promise
- People who want information without action
- People unwilling to write rules—and keep them
- People with a spreadsheet of numbers who feel tracking without interpretation is ok

The promise:

By the time you finish, you will have:

- A Levels 0-6 Cushion Map of your real assets
- Written liquidation rules you can follow when life gets emotional
- A 100-year family commitment and a series of review dates on the calendar

You don't have to do everything at once.
You just have to start building cushions with intention.

How to Use This Workbook

This workbook is designed to be used — not just read. Every fill-in line, every worksheet, every note page, every declaration page exists for one purpose: to convert the framework you are learning into a personal plan that belongs to you and your family.

Here is how to get the most out of it.

Start at Section Zero

Do not skip the HUELOC section. Before any asset can be built, the builder must be developed. Section Zero establishes the foundation that funds everything above it. Take it seriously.

Write in this workbook

Every fill-in line is an invitation to commit. Make copies. Vague intentions do not build wealth — written commitments do. Just as you write your goals or annual 'New Year's resolution. Use this workbook with a pen/pencil in hand. Be specific. Name names. Set dates. The reader who completes every page will finish with a financial plan more detailed and more personal than anything a financial advisor has ever handed them. This will make it easy to complete various trusts and estate plan language.

Return to it

This is not a workbook you complete once and shelve. Come back to it annually. Review your build plans. Update your liquidation conditions. Add new assets to your inventory. Watch the cushions grow. Your net worth will continue to grow, and your assets will be much stronger than your liabilities.

Use it with your family

The most powerful use of this workbook is as a family document. Sit down with your spouse, your children, and your trusted inner circle. Complete the generational commitment sections together. Sign the declarations together. The wealth you are building belongs to all of them.

Use it in the Masterclass

Each section of this workbook corresponds to a module in the Levels of Liquidity masterclass, live workshop, and online course. If you are working through this as part of a course, your facilitator will guide you section by section. Each worksheet is a class exercise. Each declaration is a course milestone.

A Note on the Levels

The levels in this framework are not judgments.
There is no shame in Level 1.
Every person in this workbook started at the chair.
The goal is not to rush to Level 6 — it is to build every level with intention, to know what each asset is for, and to never liquidate the wrong cushion for the wrong reason at the wrong time.
Build slowly. Build permanently. Keep the cushions on the chair.

The framework at a glance—six levels of liquidity

This workbook is organized around six levels of liquidity.
Each level is a cushion. Each cushion has a purpose.

Level 1 — Liquid (checking, cash — daily life)
Level 2 — Reserve (savings, emergency fund)
Level 3 — Self-Liquidating (royalties, dividends—income without selling)
Level 4 — Foundational (life insurance, gold, retirement accounts)
Level 5 — Next Generation (land, business — leverage never sell)
Level 6 — Future Generation (100-year structures)

Understanding what each level is for—and what it is NOT for—is the foundation of everything that follows. Remember, all levels are fed by income that converts to assets, then to wealth!

You will learn the full framework in Section Two.
You will build it across every section after that.

QUICK START

Build One Cushion Today (15 Minutes)

This workbook works best when you get a win early.
So here it is: one small decision that starts momentum.

Step 1—Name the "chair" pressure (1 sentence)
Right now, money feels heavy in our home because:

Step 2—Choose the value you're building for (circle one)

Peace • Freedom • Stability • Legacy • Giving • Opportunity • Other

Step 3—Assign levels to 3 real things you already have

Level 1 (daily spending/bills)

Level 2 (reserve/emergency):

Level 3 (royalties, residuals, dividends, etc)

Level 4 (long-term foundation):

QUICK START

Step 4 — Write one "WE WILL NOT" rule (this protects your future) We will not touch ______________________________for (Example: "We will not touch Level 2 for holidays.")

Step 5 — Choose one 7-day build action (tiny win, real progress) example: AI training, new certifications - things that could make money now or in the future.
This week, we will do ONE of the following: Transfer $______________________________ to Level 2 Cancel one leak: ______________________________ Build our HUELOC for 60 minutes (skill/credential/network): ______________________________ ______________________________

Step 6 — Accountability (optional but powerful)
We will share this rule with ______________________________ by (date): ______________________ We will review this Quick Start again on (date):______________________

THE LEVELS MAP

The Chair & The Cushions

The chair = your starting point.
The cushions = the assets you build with intention.

Level 0 — Human Equity (The Builder)
Skills • credentials • discipline • reputation • relationships

Level 1 — Liquid (Daily)
Checking • cash • debit
Purpose: daily living | Rule: spend here first

Level 2 — Reserve (Emergency)
Savings • emergency fund • money market
Purpose: protect your household | Rule: replenish immediately after use

Level 3 — Self-Liquidating (The Drip)
Royalties • dividends • IP income • annuities/pensions
Purpose: income without selling | Rule: route the drip upward—don't consume it

Level 4 — Foundation (Long-term)
Retirement accounts/equities • real estate (long hold) • gold • cash-value insurance
Purpose: compounding + protection | Rule: touch only with written intent

Level 5 — Next Generation (Never Sell)
Land • family business • Art/heirlooms/collectibles - legacy structures
Purpose: transfer, leverage, permanence | Rule: not built for you alone

Level 6 — Future Generation (100-Year Container)
Trust/foundation/structure + long-horizon assets
Purpose: institutional permanence | Rule: protect the mission

Three questions before every decision

✓ Which level does this money belong to?
✓ Am I building a cushion—or removing one?
✓ Would I make this decision in writing, with my name on it?

MY NEXT 90 DAYS

Build, Protect, Repeat

You don't close a 100-year gap in one dramatic move.
You close it with repeatable decisions.

Level 1 habit (daily discipline):
One change we will make this week

Level 2 goal (reserve):

Current Level 2 total: $

90-day target Level 2 total: $

Weekly or monthly build amount: $

Level 3 build (the drip):

The income stream we're building (or improving):

First step we will take in the next 14 days:

My NEXT 90 DAYS

One "WE WILL NOT" protection rule (cushion integrity):

We will not touch ____

for ____

Our next household review

Review date: ____

Time: ____

Who will be present:

____

What we will review:
- Levels Map updates
- Level 2 progress
- Liquidation rules
- Next build step
- One celebration

Annual review (this is how wealth becomes tradition)

Annual review month:

____

Annual review date (set now):

____

One professional we will consult this year (if applicable):

____

A cushion is built when a decision becomes a habit.

SECTIONZERO
THE HUMAN EQUITY LINE OF CREDIT

ZERO

THE HUMAN EQUITY LINE OF CREDIT

Before you can build a cushion, you must build a builder. The most powerful asset you will ever own is not a piece of land, not a life insurance policy, not a portfolio of stocks. It is you—developed, skilled, disciplined, and connected. This is Level 0. It is where everything begins.

Every level in this framework is funded by something. Level 1 is funded by income. Income is generated by work. A human being performs work. That human being—their skills, their knowledge, their discipline, their reputation, their relationships—is the engine that makes every other level possible.

This is what Steven E. LaBroi named the Human Equity Line of Credit in his book Build Your Human Equity Line of Credit. It is not a metaphor. It is a framework for understanding that the investment you make in yourself — or the investment a parent makes in a child — is the foundational asset that produces all other assets. It cannot be taxed away, repossessed, or inflated into worthlessness. It grows every time it is used. And unlike every other asset in this workbook, it is the one asset that no economic condition — not recession, not depression, not crisis — can fully liquidate.

Section Zero is the first section of this workbook for a reason. You cannot manage what you have not built. And you cannot build with intention until you understand that you — the human being reading these words — are already an asset. The question is whether you are investing in that asset the way you would invest in any other.

WHAT IS THE HUMAN EQUITY LINE OF CREDIT?

The HUELOC is the total value of your human capital — the accumulated sum of your education, skills, experiences, discipline, relationships, reputation, and knowledge — expressed as a line of credit that you draw on throughout your lifetime to generate income, create opportunities, and fund every financial level above it.

Like a financial line of credit, the HUELOC has a limit that can be raised by investing in it. A person who has invested in education, mentorship, skill development, and meaningful relationships has a high HUELOC. A person who has coasted on natural talent without development has a low one — regardless of what they currently earn.

And like every asset in this framework, the HUELOC must be built continuously. You do not develop your human capital once and stop. You build it every year, every decade, across your entire lifetime — because the world changes, markets change, and the human being who was adequate in 2010 may be obsolete in 2030 without continuous reinvestment.

The Four Functions of the HUELOC

FUNCTION 1 —

DONATIONS (INVESTING IN YOURSELF)

The HUELOC is funded by investment — in education, training, mentorship, books, courses, travel, and experiences that build skill and perspective. Every dollar spent developing a human being is a deposit. Every hour of learning is a deposit. Every relationship cultivated with someone wiser, more experienced, or more connected than you is a deposit.

This is what parents do when they invest in a child's education, expose them to culture and travel, put instruments in their hands, books on their shelves, and mentors in their path. They are not spending money. They are making the highest-yield investment available — into a human asset that will compound for seventy or eighty years.

FUNCTION 2 —

EMERGENCY RESERVE (EARNING THROUGH CRISIS)

When every financial cushion is thin — when Level 1 and Level 2 are depleted, when a recession hits, when a personal crisis strips the financial foundation — the person who has invested in their human capital can earn their way back. Skills do not disappear in a downturn. Knowledge does not evaporate in a bear market.

The Four Functions of the HUELOC

FUNCTION 3 –

SAVINGS (COMPOUNDING SKILLS AND RELATIONSHIPS)

Human capital compounds. A skill learned at twenty becomes expertise at forty. A relationship built at thirty becomes a network of opportunity at fifty. A reputation built over a decade becomes a door that opens without knocking.

FUNCTION 4 –

RISK MANAGEMENT (DIVERSIFIED HUMAN CAPITAL AS THE ULTIMATE HEDGE)

The most financially vulnerable person is the one whose income depends entirely on a single skill in a single industry for a single employer. The HUELOC framework requires diversification – not just of financial assets, but of human capital itself. Multiple income-generating skills. The ability to teach what you know. Relationships across industries and communities. Intellectual property that generates income without your active presence.

My HUELOC Inventory

Complete this inventory honestly. Your Human Equity Line of Credit is your starting point — the asset you bring to every financial decision.

My primary skill (the one I could earn from today)	
My secondary skill (a second income source if needed):	
My professional reputation (what I am known for):	
My strongest relationship asset (who opens doors for me):	
My intellectual property (what I know that others would pay to learn):	
The skill gap costing me the most income right now:	
The relationship I need to build in the next 12 months:	
My estimated annual earning capacity at current HUELOC level: $	
My estimated annual earning capacity if I close my skill gap: $	

My HUELOC build plan

The education or training I will invest in this year	
Budget allocated to my human capital this year: $	
The mentor or advisor I will seek out:	
The book, course, or certification I will complete by (date):	
The skill I will develop to create a Level 3 self-liquidating asset:	
My HUELOC investment in my child / young adult (if applicable):	
Budget allocated to their human capital development this year:	

The HUELOC Declaration

I understand that I am an asset.

Before I invest in any financial instrument, I commit to investing in myself —in my skills, my knowledge, my relationships, and my capacity to create value.

I commit to treating my child's development as the highest-yield investment available to me — because the human being I am building will compound for the next seventy years.

The cushions I stack on the chair are only as strong as the person placing them.
I am building that person too.

Signed: ___________________________________

Date: _____________________________________

GUIDED REFLECTION
THE CUSHION INTEGRITY CHECK

THE CUSHION WE'RE MOST TEMPTED TO REMOVE IS:

____

____

____

WHY? (STRESS, CELEBRATION, COMPARISON, FEAR, URGENCY):

____

____

____

THE MOMENT WE USUALLY BREAK OUR PLAN IS WHEN:

____

____

____

ONE RULE THAT WOULD PROTECT US IN THAT MOMENT:

"We will not touch ______________________________
for ______________________________."

We will do______________________________
instead:______________________________

WHO CAN HOLD US ACCOUNTABLE WITHOUT SHAME?

____

____

____

HOW WILL WE ASK THEM

____

____

____

©2026 All rights reserved – Levels of Liquidity

SECTION ONE
THE CHAIR

ONE THE CHAIR

You know that chair. The one with the splinter in the back left leg. The one where you had to sit just right, shift your weight a certain way, or you'd feel it every time. Maybe it was in your grandmother's kitchen. Maybe it was the only chair at the table. That chair was.

This workbook is about cushions.

Every asset you build — every savings account, every piece of land, every life insurance policy, every royalty check, every ounce of gold — is a cushion you place on top of that chair. The first cushion helps a little. You still feel the splinters, still feel the nails, but it's less. The second cushion helps more. By the time you have four, five, six cushions stacked — each one intentionally built, each one with a purpose and a plan — you have stopped feeling the chair entirely.

You are sitting comfortably. And your children? They may never know the chair was there.

That is the vision of this workbook. Not just your comfort. Not just your retirement. Four to five generations from now — one hundred years into the future — a family carries your name forward, never feeling the wood you started on, because you decided to stack cushions with intention.

Couple Script—12-Minute Money Peace Check-In

Set a timer for 12 minutes. Sit side-by-side. No blame. No speeches. Just clarity.

One win we had this week/month:

....

....

One pressure we're feeling right now:

....

....

One cushion we built (even small):

....

....

One cushion we protected (a "no" we honored):

....

....

One decision we need to make calmly:

....

....

One next step we will take in the next 7 days:

....

....

"We're building cushions. We're building peace. We're building this together."

SECTION TWO

What Is a Level of Liquidity?

TWO

WHAT IS A LEVEL OF LIQUIDITY?

Touch 2 of 3 — The full framework

In How to Use This Workbook you saw the framework at a glance.
Now you learn it completely — all six levels, the rules, and the principles that govern every financial decision you will make from this point forward.
Read carefully. This is the architecture everything else is built on.

Liquidity is simply how quickly and easily an asset can be converted to cash. A checking account is highly liquid — you can spend it today. A piece of land is not liquid — selling it takes time, negotiation, and paperwork.
But here is what most financial education misses: liquidity is not just a description. It is a decision. When you assign a level to an asset, you are declaring its purpose. You are deciding in advance what that asset is for — and what it is not for.

The five levels

Think of each level as a cushion on the chair. The lower levels are thinner — they exist for daily life and emergencies. The upper levels are thicker — they are harder to compress, and the highest level is never removed at all.

The Five Levels

Level 1: Liquid

Assets:

Checking accounts · Cash · Debit

Purpose:

Daily and monthly living expenses

Rule:

This is your first line. Spend from here for groceries, bills, gas.
Never skip this level to reach a higher one.

Level 2: Reserve

Assets:

Savings accounts · Money market · Emergency fund

Purpose:

Unexpected needs · 3-6 months of expenses

Rule:

This cushion absorbs emergencies. Replenish it immediately after use.

Level 3: Self-liquidating

Assets:

Royalties · Intellectual property · Dividends · Annuities

Purpose:

Assets that pay you without being sold

Rule:

These assets drip income. Route that income upward into stronger levels. Never spend the drip — build with it.

Level 4a: Life Insurance — Your Private Bank

Assets:

Whole life • Indexed Universal Life (IUL) • Cash value policies

Purpose:

Tax-advantaged growth • Family banking • Generational transfer

Rule:

You fund this continuously and borrow against it — never sell it.

The Five Levels

Level 4b: Foundational

Assets:
Gold • Real estate • Retirement accounts (401k / IRA)

Purpose:
Long-term wealth accumulation • Inflation protection

Rule:
Touch these only for defined, major life goals.

Level 5: Next Generation Asset

Assets:
Land • Family business • Life insurance death benefit • Dynasty trust assets

Purpose:
Assets committed to future generations — not to be liquidated in your lifetime

Rule:
This is the thickest cushion. It does not exist for you. A written commitment is required.

The dual-level principle

An asset does not have to live at only one level. The level is not fixed by the asset type. It is fixed by your written declaration of intent. That declaration can be updated. What cannot happen is an unconscious, unconsidered liquidation. Every movement of a cushion must be deliberate, documented, and purposeful.

Couple Script— The "Before We Spend" Pause

Use this before any unplanned purchase or any decision made under emotion.

Which level would money come from?

....

....

Would we make this decision in writing, with our name on it?

YES

NO

If "No," what do we do instead (delay, discuss, reroute)

....

....

When will we revisit this decision? (date/time)

....

....

GUIDED REFLECTION
VALUES CHECK

A strong money plan is not only numbers. It is alignment.
When our spending reflects our values, peace increases.

IN OUR HOME, MONEY IS FOR (CHOOSE UP TO 3):

- peace
- safety
- freedom
- generosity
- opportunity
- legacy
- learning

ONE SPENDING HABIT THAT DOES NOT MATCH OUR VALUES IS:

____

____

WHAT VALUE IS BEING CHALLENGED?_

____

____

ONE NEW HABIT THAT DOES MATCH OUR VALUES IS:

____

____

Start date: ______________________________

WHEN WE FEEL PRESSURE, OUR DEFAULT WILL BE:

- pause
- reflect
- talk together
- check the rules
- call a mentor/advisor

ONE SENTENCE WE WILL USE WHEN TEMPTATION SHOWS UP:

"Our cushions come first."

OUR VERSION:

____

SECTION THREE

The Tax Illusion

THREE THE TAX ILLUSION

Warning: This section may be uncomfortable. It is meant to be. The Tax Illusion is one of the most expensive mistakes wealth builders make—and it is rarely talked about directly.

Our society is built on consumption. Every advertisement, every social pressure, every cultural signal tells us to spend — to upgrade, to display, to celebrate by buying. This current runs so deep that even people who are intentionally building wealth get caught in it.

But there is a more subtle trap than pure consumerism, and it is called The Tax Illusion.

What is The Tax Illusion?

The Tax Illusion is when you mistake a tax deduction for wealth building.
A deduction reduces what you owe. It does not build a cushion.

Here is how it appears in real life:

- Someone buys a luxury vehicle because it qualifies for a business deduction. But the vehicle depreciates, requires insurance, fuel, maintenance, and tags. The tax benefit is a fraction of the total cost. They added a liability and called it a strategy.
- Someone purchases equipment, furniture, or technology they did not need — before December 31 — to reduce their taxable income. The money is gone. The stuff depreciates. No cushion was built.
- Someone gives to charity not out of generational vision but to reduce a tax bill — and selects causes without strategic purpose or family alignment.

None of these are illegal. Some are even reasonable in isolation. The problem is when the tax tail wags the wealth dog — when the goal becomes minimizing taxes rather than building assets. A deduction saves you a percentage of what you spend. A cushion compounds for generations.

The protection system — legitimate tax structures

Revocable living trust

Keeps Level 1-2 assets out of probate. Your family accesses liquid assets immediately at your death, without court intervention. Becomes irrevocable — and therefore a permanent protection — the moment you pass.

Irrevocable trust

Removes assets from your taxable estate permanently. Level 4 assets placed here are shielded from estate taxes and creditors. You give up control, but you gain permanent protection.

Dynasty trust

Protects Level 5 assets across multiple generations — in some states, indefinitely. The cushion stays on the chair long after you are gone.

Charitable Remainder Trust (CRT)

Allows you to transfer appreciated assets, receive income during your lifetime, reduce estate taxes, and leave the remainder to a charity or foundation. A strategic giving tool, not a tax illusion.

Private foundation / Ministry structure

Assets transferred into a private foundation operate outside personal taxation while serving a mission you define. This is generational philanthropy with strategic purpose — not a reflex deduction.

Private Member Association (PMA)

Operates outside many standard regulatory frameworks, allowing certain transactions and asset arrangements not available in conventional business structures. Requires proper legal guidance.

LLC / Holding company

Separates your personal assets from business liabilities. Protects Level 3 and 4 assets from business risk. The foundation of a proper asset protection strategy.

Important note: Some of the structures mentioned in this section (trusts, foundations, ministry entities, and private associations) have specific legal requirements and can be misunderstood or misused if they are set up incorrectly.

This workbook is not offering legal or tax advice, and it is not encouraging anyone to avoid lawful regulation or obligations. Consider these examples as categories of protection strategies, and consult a qualified estate attorney and tax professional to confirm what is appropriate, compliant, and wise for your situation. The goal is not shortcuts—the goal is legitimate structure, clear intent, and long-term stewardship.

Your action item

Before you complete Section Five (the Build Plan), consult with a qualified estate attorney or financial strategist about which of these structures is most appropriate for your current asset level. The workbook gives you the vision. The professional gives you the architecture.

SECTION FOUR
My Asset Inventory

FOUR MY ASSET INVENTORY

Before you can assign a level to anything, you have to see everything. Most people have never written down every asset they own in one place. This is where that changes.

List every asset below. For each one, assign a level (1 through 5), write your purpose for holding it, and write the condition — if any — under which you would liquidate it. If a Level 5 asset has no liquidation condition, write: None. I am building this for future generations.

Build Plan: GOLD/ SILVER	
Why I hold it:	
Current value:	
My target value:	
How I will build it:	
How often I add to it:	
Level assigned	
Dual-level option (if any):	

Build Plan: LIFE INSURANCE POLICY	
Why I hold it:	
Current value:	
My target value:	
How I will build it:	
How often I add to it:	
Level assigned	
Dual-level option (if any):	

BUILD PLAN: 401K / RETIREMENT ACCOUNT	
Why I hold it:	
Current value:	
My target value:	
How I will build it:	
How often I add to it:	
Level assigned	
Dual-level option (if any):	

Build Plan: STOCKS / EQUITIES	
Why I hold it:	
Current value:	
My target value:	
How I will build it:	
How often I add to it:	
Level assigned	
Dual-level option (if any):	

BUILD PLAN: REAL ESTATE	
Why I hold it:	
Current value:	
My target value:	
How I will build it:	
How often I add to it:	
Level assigned	
Dual-level option (if any):	

BUILD PLAN: ART / ARTIFACTS / MEMORABILIA	
Why I hold it:	
Current value:	
My target value:	
How I will build it:	
How often I add to it:	
Level assigned	
Dual-level option (if any):	

BUILD PLAN: MY ASSET	
Why I hold it:	
Current value:	
My target value:	
How I will build it:	
How often I add to it:	
Level assigned	
Dual-level option (if any):	

Legacy doesn't start with millions. It starts with decisions that repeat.

GUIDED REFLECTION
FAMILY LEGACY, MADE SIMPLE

IF OUR GRANDCHILDREN COULD THANK US FOR ONE FINANCIAL DECISION, IT WOULD BE:

___

___

___

THE CUSHION WE WANT TO PROTECT NO MATTER WHAT IS:

___

___

___

THE FAMILY HABIT WE WANT TO PASS DOWN:

- [ ] automatic saving
- [ ] family meetings
- [ ] skill-building
- [ ] giving
- [ ] investing
- [ ] ownership

ONE TRADITION WE WILL START THIS YEAR (SIMPLE AND REPEATABLE):

___

___

___

NEXT FAMILY MONEY CHECK-IN SCHEDULED FOR:

___

SECTION FIVE
My Build Plan

FIVE MY BUILD PLAN

You have inventoried your assets. Now you build them — deliberately, intentionally, and with a written plan for each one.

A build plan is not a wish. It is a written commitment that names the asset, declares its purpose, sets a target, and defines how you will fund it consistently. Every asset in this workbook deserves a plan. Every plan deserves your name on it.

The Build Principle

Every asset must be fed continuously.
A cushion that is not being grown is being eroded by inflation, time, and circumstance.
Your build plan is the commitment you make to keep stacking.
Write it. Sign it. Return to it every year.

Complete a build plan for every asset you hold or intend to build.

A build plan on paper becomes a cushion in life.
But only when the commitment is honored.

GUIDED REFLECTION
MY BUILD COMMITMENT

THE ASSET I AM MOST COMMITTED TO BUILDING THIS YEAR IS:

____

____

CURRENT VALUE: $ ____________________

MY 12-MONTH TARGET: $ ____________________

THE ONE ACTION I WILL TAKE THIS WEEK TOWARD IT:

____

____

THE BIGGEST OBSTACLE I EXPECT IS:

____

____

MY PLAN TO STAY ON TRACK WHEN THAT OBSTACLE SHOWS UP:

____

____

____

WHO WILL I SHARE THIS COMMITMENT WITH:

____

BY (DATE): ____________________

SECTION SIX

My Liquidation Conditions

SIX MY LIQUIDATION CONDITIONS

This section is where the discipline lives. Anyone can list assets. The wealth builder is the one who decides — in writing, in advance, when calm and clear-headed — under what conditions each asset can be touched.

Decisions made in a crisis are rarely optimal. Decisions made in advance — and honored in a crisis — are the ones that protect generational wealth.

The pull order — always start at the top of the stack

- An everyday expense → Level 1 (liquid) first.
- An unexpected emergency → Level 2 (reserve) before anything else.
- A defined major goal → Level 3 or Level 2 investment assets, with a written reason.
- A transformational generational opportunity → Level 4 may be considered, with full family discussion and documentation.
- Level 5 → Never. Not in your lifetime. That is the promise you are making.

My written liquidation rules

Complete the following for each asset. Be specific. Vague rules are not honored under pressure.

Checking / Cash (Level 1)

I will liquidate this asset when:

....

....

I will NOT liquidate this asset for:

....

....

Before liquidating, I will first consult:

....

....

Savings/ Emergency fund (Level 2)

I will liquidate this asset when:

....

....

I will NOT liquidate this asset for:

....

....

Before liquidating, I will first consult:

....

....

Stocks / Investments (Level 2–3)Checking / Cash (Level 1)

I will liquidate this asset when:

....

....

I will NOT liquidate this asset for:

....

....

Before liquidating, I will first consult:

....

....

Gold (Level 4b)

I will liquidate this asset when:

....

....

I will NOT liquidate this asset for:

....

....

Before liquidating, I will first consult:

....

....

Life insurance — cash value (Level 4a)

I will liquidate this asset when:

....

....

I will NOT liquidate this asset for:

....

....

Before liquidating, I will first consult:

....

....

Real estate (Level 4–5)

I will liquidate this asset when:

....

....

I will NOT liquidate this asset for:

....

....

Before liquidating, I will first consult:

....

....

Retirement accounts (Level 4)

I will liquidate this asset when:

....

....

I will NOT liquidate this asset for:

....

....

Before liquidating, I will first consult:

....

....

Land (Level 5)

I will liquidate this asset when:

....

....

I will NOT liquidate this asset for:

....

....

Before liquidating, I will first consult:

....

....

Business ownership (Level 4–5)

I will liquidate this asset when:

....

....

I will NOT liquidate this asset for:

....

....

Before liquidating, I will first consult:

....

....

Business ownership (Level 4–5)

I will liquidate this asset when:

....

....

I will NOT liquidate this asset for:

....

....

Before liquidating, I will first consult:

....

....

My asset: ____________________ (Level ___)

I will liquidate this asset when:

....

....

I will NOT liquidate this asset for:

....

....

Before liquidating, I will first consult:

....

....

My asset: ____________________ (Level ___)

I will liquidate this asset when:

....

....

I will NOT liquidate this asset for:

....

....

Before liquidating, I will first consult:

....

....

My asset: ____________________ (Level ___)

I will liquidate this asset when:

....

....

I will NOT liquidate this asset for:

....

....

Before liquidating, I will first consult:

....

....

My asset: ____________________ (Level ___)

I will liquidate this asset when:

....

....

I will NOT liquidate this asset for:

....

....

Before liquidating, I will first consult:

....

....

SECTION SEVEN
My Economy Playbook

SEVEN

MY ECONOMY PLAYBOOK

Economies change. Markets grow, stall, contract, and sometimes collapse. Most people make their worst financial decisions during economic downturns — not because they are careless, but because nobody ever gave them a pre-written plan for which cushion to pull from first.

This section is that plan. You write it now, when you are clear. You follow it when the pressure comes.

My personal economy rules

In a growth economy, I will build:

....

....

....

In a recession, my first pull will be:

....

....

....

The asset I will never sell regardless of the economy:

....

....

The person I will consult before any major liquidation:

....

....

Community Check-In (10 Minutes)

This workbook works best with encouragement.

One cushion I'm building right now:

....

....

....

One rule I'm practicing:

....

....

....

One challenge I'm facing (no details needed):

....

....

....

One step I'm taking this week:

....

....

....

One person who can check on me:

....

....

....

SECTION EIGHT

The Next Generation Commitment

EIGHT THE NEXT GENERATION COMMITMENT

Most books talk about your retirement. This one talks about your great-great-grandchildren. The chair you started on — they may never know it existed. That is the goal. One hundred years. Four to five generations. A family that inherits cushions, not starting points.

The Next Generation Commitment is the most important section in this workbook. It is not a financial calculation. It is a declaration. It is you deciding — in writing — what you are building, who it is for, and what it will mean one century from now.

My personal economy rules

In 100 years, I want my family to

....

....

The asset I most want to still be in our family

....

....

The value I most want to pass down (beyond money)

....

....

The generation I am most building for

....

....

My Level 5 commitments

For each Level 5 asset, complete the commitment below. This is your declaration. Sign it. Date it. Share it with someone who will hold you to it.

Level 5 Asset # 1	
Asset Name / Description	
Current Estimated Value	
Protection Structure (trust, LLC, etc.)	
Who it passes to	
What it will mean to them	
Condition under which it could ever be touched	
If none — write it: 'None. This asset is not mine to spend.'	

Level 5 Asset # 2	
Asset Name / Description	
Current Estimated Value	
Protection Structure (trust, LLC, etc.)	
Who it passes to	
What it will mean to them	
Condition under which it could ever be touched	
If none — write it: 'None. This asset is not mine to spend.'	

Level 5 Asset # 3	
Asset Name / Description	
Current Estimated Value	
Protection Structure (trust, LLC, etc.)	
Who it passes to	
What it will mean to them	
Condition under which it could ever be touched	
If none — write it: 'None. This asset is not mine to spend.'	

My declaration

I,.., declare that I am building assets with intention.

I understand that every asset has a purpose. Every level has a strategy. Every generation has a plan.

I commit to building my cushions—not just for my comfort, but for the family that will sit in the chair one hundred years from now, and never feel the wood I started on.

Signed: .... Date: ....

Witness: .... Date: ....

SECTION NINE

My Level 6 Vision — 100 Years Forward

NINE

MY LEVEL 6 VISION — 100 YEARS FORWARD

Most books are written for who you are today. This section is written for who your family will be one hundred years from now. Level 6 is not a financial strategy. It is a declaration of permanence.

Every level below this one was built for people you know — for you, your children, your grandchildren. Level 6 is built for people whose names you will never know, whose faces you will never see, who will live in a world you cannot fully imagine.

That is exactly why it must be built now.

What belongs at Level 6

- **Digital currency and cryptocurrency** — held inside a trust or foundation, never a personal wallet
- **Global business interests** — stakes in international ventures, emerging markets, cross-border enterprises
- **Higher-risk growth ventures** — early-stage companies, private equity, innovation-sector investments
- **Emerging asset classes** — tokenized real estate, digital IP, AI-generated assets, technologies not yet named
- **The 508(c)(1)(a) structure itself** — your ministry as an asset-holding and deploying institution
- **The family PMA** — your private contractual community operating its own economy inside a legal shield

The Level 6 funding sequence

Establish the legal structure (trust, 508c1a, PMA, foundation, dynasty trust)

Write the family charter — mission, values, distribution rules, governance across generations

Fund with proceeds from Level 3 self-liquidating income and Level 5 refinancing

Acquire Level 6 assets inside the structure — never in your personal name

Name successor trustees or directors across at least two future generations

Review and update the charter every 10 years — the world will change; the mission should not

My Level 6 legal structure		
Structure type (trust / 508c1a / PMA / foundation / other):		
Name of the structure		
Attorney / advisor building it		
Target date to establish		
First asset to place inside it		
Funding source (Level 3 income/Level 5 refi / other_		

My family charter — the 100-year mission

The mission of this structure in one sentence:

....

The three values that guide every decision:

1. ....
2. ....
3. ....

The first successor steward after me:

....

....

The second successor steward:

....

....

What this structure will never do:

....

....

What this structure will always do:

....

....

100 years from now, I want this structure to

....

....

Level 6 Asset # 1	
Asset type/description:	
Why it belongs at Level 6	
Target holding period:	
Structure that will hold it:	
Generation that will most benefit:	

Level 6 Asset # 2	
Asset type/description:	
Why it belongs at Level 6	
Target holding period:	
Structure that will hold it:	
Generation that will most benefit:	

Level 6 Asset # 3	
Asset type/description:	
Why it belongs at Level 6	
Target holding period:	
Structure that will hold it:	
Generation that will most benefit:	

Level 6 Asset # 4	
Asset type/description:	
Why it belongs at Level 6	
Target holding period:	
Structure that will hold it:	
Generation that will most benefit:	

Level 6 Asset # 5	
Asset type/description:	
Why it belongs at Level 6	
Target holding period:	
Structure that will hold it:	
Generation that will most benefit:	

Level 6 Asset # 6	
Asset type/description:	
Why it belongs at Level 6	
Target holding period:	
Structure that will hold it:	
Generation that will most benefit:	

My 100-year commitment

I am not building this for myself alone.

I am building a structure that will hold assets, generate resources, and serve a mission for one hundred years — for four to five generations of a family that carries my name forward.

I understand that the greatest gift I can give is not money.
It is a permanent institution, a written mission, and a legal structure
that protects and grows what I have built long after I am gone.

I commit to establishing my Level 6 structure, writing my family charter,
and naming the stewards who will carry it forward.

The chair I started on will not be the chair they sit on.
They will sit in a room I built for them.

Signed: .... Date: ....

Structure name: ....

Witness / Co-steward: ....
Date: ....

SECTION TEN

Building Your Private Family Office

TEN

BUILDING YOUR PRIVATE FAMILY OFFICE

Generational wealth is not managed alone. Every family that has built and kept wealth across generations did not do it by themselves — they built a team.
The Private Family Office is that team. It is not a physical office. It is a circle of trusted professionals, coordinated by you, guarding every dimension of the wealth you have built.

You have now completed the foundational work. You have inventoried your assets, written your build plans, declared your liquidation conditions, committed to your generational vision, and established your Level 6 structures.

What you have built is real. What you have committed to is serious. And serious wealth — wealth designed to last one hundred years — requires professional support.

THE SIX PILLARS OF THE PRIVATE FAMILY OFFICE

THE BANKER

Level connection: Levels 1, 4b, 5—credit, leverage, refinancing.

Refinancing: Your banker manages your relationship with institutional capital. They provide credit lines, commercial lending, and refinancing relationships that allow you to extract cash from Level 5 properties without selling them.

My Banker Worksheet

Name of my current Banker (or "None yet"):

....

How long we have worked together:

....

What they currently do for me:

....

What I need them to do that they are NOT doing:

....

Rating of this relationship (1-10): ....

My action – upgrade / find / deepen by (date):..

THE SIX PILLARS OF THE PRIVATE FAMILY OFFICE

THE ATTORNEY

Level connection: Levels 4-5, Level 6 — trusts, entities, protectionYour attorney is the architect of your protection structures.

They build and maintain the trusts, LLCs, foundations, PMAs, and dynasty trust structures that shield every level of your asset stack.

My Attornery Worksheet

Name of my current Attorney (or "None yet"):

....

How long we have worked together:

....

What they currently do for me:

....

What I need them to do that they are NOT doing:

....

Rating of this relationship (1-10): ....

My action — upgrade / find / deepen by (date):...

THE SIX PILLARS OF THE PRIVATE FAMILY OFFICE

THE INSURANCE EXPERT

Level connection: Level 4a — life insurance, cash value, risk transfer.

Your insurance expert designs and monitors the life insurance architecture at Level 4a — your private banking cushion and your primary Level 5 transfer vehicle.

My Insurance Expert Worksheet

Name of my current Insurance Expert (or "None yet"):

....

How long we have worked together:

....

What they currently do for me:

....

What I need them to do that they are NOT doing:

....

Rating of this relationship (1-10): ....

My action — upgrade / find / deepen by (date):...

THE SIX PILLARS OF THE PRIVATE FAMILY OFFICE

THE FINANCIAL ADVISOR

Level connection: Levels 2-4b — investments, retirement, reinvestment routingYour financial advisor manages the investment architecture of your portfolio. They are a fiduciary — legally required to act in your interest, not earn commissio

My Financial Advisor Worksheet

Name of my current Financial Advisor (or "None yet"):

....

How long we have worked together:

....

What they currently do for me:

....

What I need them to do that they are NOT doing:

....

Rating of this relationship (1-10): ....

My action — upgrade / find / deepen by (date):..

THE SIX PILLARS OF THE PRIVATE FAMILY OFFICE

THE TAX ADVISOR

Level connection: All levels — The Tax Illusion defense, structure optimizationYour tax advisor is the front-line defense against the Tax Illusion. They help you structure assets correctly so that the tax burden is minimized legitimately and permanently.

My Tax Advisor Worksheet

Name of my current Tax Advisor (or "None yet"):

....

How long we have worked together:

....

What they currently do for me:

....

What I need them to do that they are NOT doing:

....

Rating of this relationship (1-10): ....

My action — upgrade / find / deepen by (date):...

THE SIX PILLARS OF THE PRIVATE FAMILY OFFICE

FAMILY OFFICE DIRECTOR

Level connection: All levels — coordination, accountability, executionEvery wealthy family needs someone whose job is to make sure the team functions as a team — not as five separate professionals who each see only their piece of the picture.

My Family Office Director Worksheet

Name of my current Family Office Director (or "None yet"):

....

How long we have worked together:

....

What they currently do for me:

....

What I need them to do that they are NOT doing:

....

Rating of this relationship (1-10): ....

My action — upgrade / find / deepen by (date):..

PRIVATE FAMILY OFFICE ACTIVATION CHECKLIST

This is the final action page of the workbook. The commitments you make here are not aspirational. They are operational. Name names. Set dates.

Banker: ______________________________

Activated by: ______________________________

Attorney (estate/asset protection): ______________________________

Activated by: ______________________________

Insurance Expert: ______________________________

Activated by: ______________________________

Financial Advisor (fiduciary): ______________________________

Activated by ______________________________

Tax Advisor / CPA: ______________________________

Activated by: ______________________________

Project Manager / Family Office Director: ______________________________

Activated by: ______________________________

First team coordination meeting scheduled for: ______________________________

Annual family wealth review scheduled for: ______________________________

The vision document I will share with my team is this workbook.

Signed: ____________________________

Date: _____________________________

You have now done what most people never do.

You have looked at every asset you own, assigned it a purpose, written a plan to build it, declared when it can and cannot be touched, committed to a 100-year vision, and built the team to execute it.

The chair is still real.

But look how many cushions you have placed on it.

Keep building.

Never sit on bare wood again.

Filled Examples — How a Completed Page Looks

FOR ILLUSTRATION ONLY

These examples show what filled-in pages look like. All figures are fictional and are for illustration purposes only. Use them as a guide as you complete your own pages.

Sample 1 — Asset Inventory (Excerpt)

Asset: Checking Account (Household Bills)

Current Value: $2,400

Level Assigned: Level 1 — Liquid

Purpose: bills, groceries, gas

Liquidation Condition: normal monthly spending

Will NOT liquidate for: vacations, gifts, impulse purchases

Consult Before Major Change: spouse/partner

Asset: Emergency Savings

Current Value: $5,000

Level Assigned: Level 2 — Reserve

Purpose: job loss, medical, urgent repairs

Liquidation Condition: true emergency only

Will NOT liquidate for: holidays, lifestyle upgrades

Consult Before Using: spouse/partner + one trusted mentor

Asset: 401(k)

Current Value: $38,000

Level Assigned: Level 4 — Foundational

Purpose: long-term compounding for later life

Liquidation Condition: only if written plan allows and alternatives are exhausted

Will NOT liquidate for: consumer purchases

Consult Before: fiduciary advisor / CPA (if applicable)

Sample 1 — Asset Inventory (Excerpt)

Build Plan: Emergency Fund (Level 2)

Why I hold it: household peace + protection

Current value: $5,000

My target value: $18,000 (6 months of essential expenses)

How I will build it: automatic transfer after each paycheck

How often I add to it: every payday

Level assigned: Level 2

Dual-level option (if any): none — this is protection only

Signature commitment: I will protect this cushion because panic is expensive—and peace is priceless.

Signed: ______________________________________

Date: ______________________________________

Sample 3 — Liquidation Rules (Excerpt)

Savings / Emergency Fund (Level 2)

I will liquidate this asset when: medical emergency, job loss, essential car/home repair

I will NOT liquidate this asset for: holidays, vacations, gifts, lifestyle upgrades

Before liquidating, I will first consult: my spouse/partner and one trusted mentor

Gold / Long-term store of value (Level 4)

I will liquidate this asset when: a once-in-a-generation opportunity aligns with our written plan

I will NOT liquidate this asset for: temporary emergencies that Level 2 can cover

Before liquidating, I will first consult: spouse/partner + advisor (if applicable)

Sample 4 — My Economy Playbook Answers

Build Plan: Emergency Fund (Level 2)

Why I hold it: household peace + protection

Current value: $5,000

My target value: $18,000 (6 months of essential expenses)

How I will build it: automatic transfer after each paycheck

How often I add to it: every payday

Level assigned: Level 2

Dual-level option (if any): none — this is protection only

Signature commitment: I will protect this cushion because panic is expensive—and peace is priceless.

Signed: ____________________________________

Date: ____________________________________

CASE STUDIES

Case Studies — Walking Through the Levels

Fictional composite for teaching purposes. Not financial, legal, tax, or investment advice. Readers should adapt the clues to their own situation and consult qualified professionals where appropriate.

Case Studies

The Levels of Liquidity framework becomes clearer when you can see it in motion. The following case studies are fictional composites created for teaching purposes.

They do not represent financial advice, legal advice, tax advice, investment advice, or guaranteed outcomes.

They are examples of how different people and households might use this workbook to assign purpose to assets, build cushions, write liquidation rules, and create a legacy plan that fits their actual lives.

Each story begins in a different place. The process is the same: see what you have, name what it is for, build it with intention, and protect it before pressure arrives

How to Use These Case Studies

- Read the profile that feels closest to your situation first.
- Circle the clue that sounds like your household, even if the numbers are different.
- Use the Starting Cushion Map to help you fill in your own Levels Map.
- Borrow the language of the "We Will Not Touch" rule and make it personal.
- Use the 90-Day Build Plan as a model for your own next step.

Case Study Overview

Marcus — Single Male Professional

The Focus: Curbing lifestyle inflation and establishing financial structure.

The Outline: Identifies how unallocated high income gets absorbed by lifestyle creep; walks through assigning names and strict boundary rules to his savings; outlines leveraging cybersecurity expertise to build a Level 3 self-liquidating asset.

Danielle — Single Female Professional

The Focus: Balancing personal independence with family caregiving.

The Outline: Tackles the pressure of being the default "emergency plan" for others; details how to build clear financial boundaries around a personal reserve; outlines transitioning from spontaneous handouts to structured, planned giving and legacy mentorship.

Jordan and Maya — Young Professional Couple

The Focus: Establishing household alignment before facing major financial pressure.

The Outline: Solves the tension of making isolated purchase decisions instead of following a unified plan; introduces communication tools like the "12-Minute Money Peace Check-In," and outlines balancing debt payoff with building a shared family reserve.

Case Study Overview

The Thompsons — Blue-Collar Family with Children

The Focus: Protecting hourly and variable income with small, consistent cushions.

The Outline: Addresses the cycle of surprise bills wiping out months of hard work; removes the shame of starting small ($25 automatic transfers); outlines how to define strict liquidation conditions and involve children in building a family asset binder.

Renee — Entrepreneur

The Focus: Managing business cash flow, tax discipline, and building transferable legacy architecture.

The Outline: Resolves the "feast or famine" emotional cycle of business revenue; details the clean separation of business and personal accounts; challenges the illusion of year-end tax deductions; outlines documenting core business systems so the asset can outlive the founder.

MARCUS

Single Male Professional

Structure before lifestyle inflation

Fictional composite for teaching purposes. Not financial, legal, tax, or investment advice. Readers should adapt the clues to their own situation and consult qualified professionals where appropriate.

Case Study 1 — Marcus: The Single Male Professional

Profile

Marcus is 36, single, and works as a cybersecurity manager.

He earns a high income, but for most of his adult life, his money has moved quickly.

He is not reckless. He is generous with family, enjoys travel, upgrades technology often, and tells himself that because he earns well, he is fine. His checking account is usually full at the beginning of the month and thinner than expected by the end.

Marcus came to the workbook with a quiet concern:

"I make more than my parents ever made, but I don't feel like I'm building more than they built."

That sentence was his chair. Not poverty. Not crisis. Not failure. His chair was the fear that a good income might turn into a good lifestyle instead of a permanent foundation.

THE CHAIR PRESSURE

Marcus's pressure was lifestyle inflation. Every raise had created a new normal. Better apartment. Better car. Better trips. Better restaurants. None of those choices were wrong by themselves, but together they had created a pattern: his income increased, and his obligations expanded to meet it.

When Marcus completed the Quick Start page, his sentence was simple:

Right now, money feels heavy because I do not know which dollars are for today and which dollars are for the future.

That sentence changed the work. Marcus did not need shame. He needed assignment. His money needed names.

His Starting Cushion Map

Level	What Marcus Had	Purpose He Assigned
Level 0 — HUELOC	Cybersecurity skills, management experience, industry relationships	Increase earning power and build future consulting/IP income
Level 1 — Liquid	Checking account with one month of expenses flowing through it	Bills, groceries, transportation, basic living
Level 2 — Reserve	$8,500 in savings	Emergency reserve only—not travel, gadgets, or gifts
Level 3 — Self-Liquidating	No current asset; idea for a cybersecurity training course	Future income without selling time hour by hour
Level 4 — Foundation	401(k), brokerage account, cash-value life insurance conversation pending	Long-term compounding and protection
Level 5 — Next Generation	No current Level 5 asset	Future land, family trust, or business interest
Level 6 — Future Generation	Not yet	A future structure once Level 3 and Level 5 become real

WHAT MARCUS LEARNED IN THE WORKBOOK

The biggest shift for Marcus came from the line: liquidity is not just a description; it is a decision. Before the workbook, he thought of money as "available" or "not available." After the workbook, he began asking: available for what?

His Level 2 savings account had been technically liquid, but spiritually confused. It was labeled "savings," but he used it for vacations, gifts, and last-minute upgrades. The workbook helped him see that if every cushion is available for every feeling, then no cushion is protected.

Marcus also saw that his HUELOC was already strong. He had valuable knowledge. He was known in his field. People asked him questions they would pay someone to answer. That realization pointed him toward Level 3: a self-liquidating asset built from expertise.

His 90-Day Build Plan

Marcus kept his first plan simple. He did not try to rebuild his entire financial life in one weekend. He wrote a 90-day plan he could actually keep.

LEVEL 1 HABIT:
create a weekly spending limit for restaurants, travel deposits, and impulse technology.

LEVEL 2 GOAL:
grow savings from $8,500 to $12,000 and rename the account "Do Not Touch Reserve."

LEVEL 3 BUILD:
outline a paid cybersecurity workshop for small business owners and record three short teaching videos.

LEVEL 4 ACTION:
increase retirement contribution by 2% and schedule a review with a qualified financial professional.

Accountability: review spending and cushion progress with his brother on the first Sunday of each month.

His first seven-day action was not dramatic. He moved $500 to Level 2 and canceled two subscriptions he had forgotten about. Then he blocked two hours on Saturday to sketch his training course. The win was not the amount. The win was obedience to the plan.

His "We Will Not Touch" Rule

Marcus wrote:

"***I will not touch Level 2 for travel, technology upgrades, dating, gifts, or lifestyle upgrades. I will only touch it for job loss, medical need, urgent family crisis, or essential repair."***

He also added a rule for his future Level 3 income:

"***When the cybersecurity course earns money, I will route the first 50% upward to Level 2 and Level 4 before I spend any of it."***

That second rule mattered. Without it, a new income stream could have become a new spending stream. With it, Marcus turned expertise into a cushion.

His Next Generation Commitment

Marcus does not have children yet, but the workbook asked him to think beyond his current household. That question stretched him. His first response was, ***"I don't know who I'm building for yet."*** Then he realized that building before the family arrives is still legacy work.

His commitment became:

I am building so the family I may have one day does not inherit my lack of structure. I will become the man who has cushions before people need to sit on them.

His possible Level 5 vision was land in the county where his grandparents had lived. Not as a fantasy purchase, but as a future commitment: something to be owned, protected, and never treated casually.

CLUES FOR THE READERS

- If your income is strong but your progress feels weak, your issue may be assignment, not ability.
- If savings is used for everything, it is not functioning as Level 2.
- If people already ask you for advice, your HUELOC may contain a Level 3 asset waiting to be built.
- If you are single, you can still build generational structure before your future household arrives.

KEY TAKEAWAYS

Marcus did not need to earn more before he could begin. He needed to stop letting every dollar live at Level 1. Once he gave each cushion a purpose, his income started becoming architecture instead of atmosphere.

DANIELLE

Single Female Professional

Independence, care, and legacy protection

Fictional composite for teaching purposes. Not financial, legal, tax, or investment advice. Readers should adapt the clues to their own situation and consult qualified professionals where appropriate.

Case Study 2 — Danielle: The Single Female Professional

Profile

Danielle is 42, single, and works as a senior healthcare administrator. She is capable, respected, and dependable. In her family, she is also the person people call when something breaks. She helps an aging parent, supports a younger niece when needed, and quietly covers gaps that other people never see.

Danielle's chair was not low income. Her chair was over-responsibility. She had built a career, but she had not built enough rules around access to her resources. Her heart was generous, but her cushions were being pulled before they had time to grow.

THE CHAIR PRESSURE

When Danielle filled out the Quick Start page, her "chair pressure" was direct:

Right now, money feels heavy because I am the emergency plan for too many people, and I do not have a written emergency plan for myself.

That sentence was difficult, but it was honest. She did not want to stop helping. She wanted to help from structure instead of exhaustion. The workbook gave her permission to separate generosity from unplanned liquidation.

Her Starting Cushion Map

Level	What Danielle Had	Purpose She Assigned
Level 0 — HUELOC	Leadership skills, healthcare operations knowledge, strong professional reputation	Protect earning power; develop consulting or speaking opportunity
Level 1 — Liquid	Checking account plus automatic bill pay	Daily life and planned giving only
Level 2 — Reserve	$14,000 emergency fund	Danielle's own household reserve first
Level 3 — Self-Liquidating	No formal asset; potential workshop on healthcare career navigation	Future income stream and mentorship tool
Level 4 — Foundation	403(b), IRA, life insurance, small brokerage account	Long-term independence and protection
Level 5 — Next Generation	Family home possibility; niece's education support vision	Legacy without losing personal stability
Level 6 — Future Generation	Not yet	Future scholarship or family education fund

WHAT DANIELLE LEARNED IN THE WORKBOOK

Danielle learned that a cushion without a boundary becomes public property. That realization was not about selfishness. It was about stewardship. If she depleted her Level 2 reserve every time someone else had a Level 1 problem, she would eventually become the person in crisis.

The Tax Illusion section also made her think differently about charitable giving. She had always given when asked, but not always with a clear purpose. She began asking: Does this giving reflect my values? Is it planned? Does it build the kind of family and community I want to support?

The HUELOC section helped Danielle see her expertise as more than employment. She had coached younger professionals for years without naming that skill. Her knowledge could become a Level 3 asset: a paid workshop, career guide, or speaking opportunity that helped others while building a cushion.

Her 90-Day Build Plan

- **Level 1 habit**: create a monthly family-support category instead of responding from checking without limits.
- **Level 2 goal:** protect $14,000 as untouchable emergency reserve and build toward $20,000.
- **Level 3 build:** outline a career-navigation workshop for young women entering healthcare administration.
- **Level 4 action:** update beneficiary designations and schedule a review of retirement and life insurance planning.
- **Level 5 action:** write a first draft of her niece education commitment without promising money she had not yet built.

Danielle's first seven-day action was a boundary conversation. She told her family, kindly, that she was creating a written plan for how she could help. She would still be generous, but she would no longer make emergency decisions in the hallway of someone else's crisis.

Her "We Will Not Touch" Rule

Danielle wrote:

"I will not touch my Level 2 reserve for non-emergency family requests, guilt, pressure, or last-minute obligations. I will help from my planned giving category first."

Then she wrote a second sentence that changed her behavior:

"If I cannot help without removing a cushion, I will pause before I promise."

This became her household sentence, even though she lived alone. A household can be one person. Peace still needs rules.

Her Next Generation Commitment

Danielle's next-generation vision centered on education, dignity, and stability. She did not want to become the relative who gave randomly until she was depleted. She wanted to become the relative who created a path.

Her commitment read:

"I want my niece and the young women coming behind me to inherit more than emergency help. I want them to inherit examples, skills, and structures."

Her first Level 5 idea was not a large asset. It was a protected education fund and a written family learning tradition: once a quarter, she would host a money-and-career dinner for younger relatives. That may not sound like an institution yet, but every institution begins as a repeated commitment.

CLUES FOR THE READERS

- If you are the dependable one, you need written rules before people need you.
- Generosity is strongest when it is planned, not pressured.
- Single does not mean unsupported; choose an accountability person before a crisis.
- Your professional knowledge may be a Level 3 asset if people already seek your guidance.

KEY TAKEAWAY

Danielle did not become less generous. She became more structured. The workbook helped her protect the builder, protect the reserve, and turn care into legacy instead of depletion.

JORDAN AND MAYA

The Young Professional Couple

Independence, care, and legacy protection

Fictional composite for teaching purposes. Not financial, legal, tax, or investment advice. Readers should adapt the clues to their own situation and consult qualified professionals where appropriate.

Case Study 3 — Jordan and Maya: The Young Professional Couple

Profile

Jordan and Maya are 31 and 29. Jordan works in logistics management. Maya is a nurse practitioner. They are newly married, dual income, and hopeful. They also carry student loans, car payments, and a quiet pressure to look like they are doing well.

They are not fighting about money every week, but money is present in the background of many conversations. One wants to save faster. The other wants to enjoy life while they are young. Both are right in part. Neither wants money to become the third voice in the marriage.

THE CHAIR PRESSURE

Their Quick Start sentence was written together:

"Right now, money feels heavy in our home because we make decisions one purchase at a time instead of one plan at a time."

That sentence gave them a shared language. The issue was not that one person was responsible and the other was careless. The issue was that they had not decided what each cushion was for before pressure arrived.

Their Starting Cushion Map

Level	What Jordan and Maya Had	Purpose They Assigned
Level 0 — HUELOC	Jordan's logistics experience; Maya's clinical skill and credentials	Protect earning power; continue education without lifestyle creep
Level 1 — Liquid	Joint checking and separate personal accounts	Bills, groceries, household spending, planned fun money
Level 2 — Reserve	$6,200 in savings	Emergency fund only; first target $15,000
Level 3 — Self-Liquidating	No current asset; Maya has interest in health education content	Future education product or workshop
Level 4 — Foundation	Two retirement accounts, life insurance through work	Long-term compounding; review coverage outside employer benefits
Level 5 — Next Generation	No asset yet; dream of rental property or land	Future family asset to protect
Level 6 — Future Generation	Not yet	Too early, but not too early to think about values

WHAT JORDAN & MAYA LEARNED IN THE WORKBOOK

The couple script became the breakthrough tool. The 12-Minute Money Peace Check-In gave them a way to talk without turning the conversation into a trial. They started sitting side-by-side at the kitchen table on Sunday evenings. The rule was simple: no blame, no speeches, just clarity.

The "Before We Spend" Pause helped them slow down unplanned purchases. They did not ban enjoyment. They gave enjoyment a level. Date nights lived in Level 1. Emergencies lived in Level 2. Future ownership lived above both. Once they could see the levels, the conversation softened.

They also learned that debt payoff and cushion-building could happen together. Their plan did not require perfection. It required order. They would keep paying debt, but they would not leave Level 2 empty while doing it.

Their 90-Day Build Plan

- **Level 1 habit:** create separate weekly spending amounts for personal fun money so every small purchase does not require a conversation.
- **Level 2 goal:** grow reserve from $6,200 to $9,500 in 90 days using automatic transfers after each paycheck.
- **Debt discipline:** continue scheduled loan payments and avoid adding new consumer debt.
- **Level 3 build:** Maya will outline three health education topics that could become a paid workshop in the future.
- **Household rhythm:** hold a 12-minute check-in every other Sunday night.

Their first seven-day action was to rename their savings account "Family Peace Reserve." That small act mattered. It reminded them what the money was for. Not punishment. Not restriction. Peace.

Their "We Will Not Touch" Rule

Together they wrote:

*"**We will not touch Level 2 for vacations, furniture upgrades, gifts, or pressure to appear successful. We will use Level 2 only for true household emergencies."***

Then they added a marriage rule:

No major unplanned purchase without the 2-minute pause.

That rule protected them from the kinds of purchases that begin with emotion and end with silence.

Their Next Generation Commitment

Jordan and Maya do not have children yet, but they want them. The workbook helped them realize that family culture begins before children arrive. Their future children would inherit not only money, but patterns. If Sunday check-ins became normal now, financial peace would one day feel normal in their home.

Their commitment was simple:

"We are building a household where money has rules, love has room, and our children do not learn financial fear as their first language."

Their Level 5 dream became a written line: a small rental property or piece of land acquired after Level 2 was fully funded and consumer debt was reduced. Writing it down made it less like fantasy and more like direction.

CLUES FOR THE READERS

- If money conversations create tension, shorten them and structure them.
- If you are a couple, build shared language before building large assets.
- Fun money works better when it is named instead of hidden.
- Your first legacy habit may be a recurring family meeting, not a trust document

KEY TAKEAWAY

Jordan and Maya did not need to choose between enjoying life and building wealth. They needed to assign enjoyment a place and protect the cushions above it. The workbook turned money from a source of tension into a shared practice.

THE THOMPSONS

Blue-Collar Family with Children

Small consistent cushions on hourly income

Fictional composite for teaching purposes. Not financial, legal, tax, or investment advice. Readers should adapt the clues to their own situation and consult qualified professionals where appropriate.

Case Study 4 — The Thompsons: The Blue-Collar Family with Children

Profile

Andre and Keisha Thompson are raising two children, ages 9 and 13. Andre is an hourly maintenance technician. Keisha works part-time at a school and manages much of the household. Their income is steady, but not always predictable. Overtime helps some months. Car repairs, school needs, and family obligations hit other months.

The Thompsons are proud people. They work hard. They give what they can. They also know the feeling of sitting on the chair: the hard place where one surprise bill can undo three months of progress.

THE CHAIR PRESSURE

Their Quick Start sentence was honest:

" Right now, money feels heavy because every time we get a little ahead, something pulls us back."

For the Thompsons, the workbook had to feel practical. They did not need a lecture about investing before they had a reserve. They needed a system that respected hourly work, children, groceries, gas, and the reality of pressure.

Their Starting Cushion Map

Level	What Jordan and Maya Had	Purpose They Assigned
Level 0 — HUELOC	Andre's repair skills, Keisha's school network, both parents' discipline	Increase income options; teach children skills early
Level 1 — Liquid	Checking account, cash envelope for groceries	Daily life and bills
Level 2 — Reserve	$750 in savings	Emergency reserve; first target $2,500
Level 3 — Self-Liquidating	None yet; possible weekend repair tutorials or small rental tools	Future income without depending only on overtime
Level 4 — Foundation	Andre's retirement plan, small life insurance policies	Long-term protection and family stability
Level 5 — Next Generation	No land or business yet	Children's HUELOC and future ownership mindset
Level 6 — Future Generation	Not yet	Values and habits first; structures later

WHAT THEY LEARNED IN THE WORKBOOK

The Thompsons needed to hear: there is no shame in Level 1. That line mattered. Many financial books make working families feel behind before they begin. This workbook gave them a starting place without insult.

They also learned that HUELOC was not only for executives. Andre's repair skill was human capital. Keisha's relationships at the school were human capital. Their children's curiosity was human capital. The family began talking about skills as assets.

The biggest shift came in Section Six: Liquidation Conditions. The family had used savings for anything urgent. The workbook helped them separate urgent from important, emergency from inconvenience, and pressure from purpose.

Their 90-Day Build Plan

- **Level 1 habit: create a weekly cash plan for groceries, gas, and school extras.**
- **Level 2 goal:** ·grow reserve from $750 to $1,500 in 90 days through automatic transfers and saving a portion of overtime.
- **HUELOC build:** Andre will pursue one employer-paid certification; Keisha will explore full-time school district opportunities.
- **Children's HUELOC:** each child will learn one practical household skill and one money habit per month.
- **Family rhythm:** one 20-minute monthly cushion meeting with the children included.

Their first seven-day action was $25 into savings and one family meeting at the dinner table. That may sound small to someone with more income. It was not small. It was the beginning of a new identity: we are a family that builds cushions

Their "We Will Not Touch" Rule

The Thompsons wrote:

"We will not touch Level 2 for fast food, school clothes that are not necessary, birthday pressure, or helping others before we check our own household plan."

They also wrote a children's version:

"Emergency money is for real emergencies. If it can wait, we wait."

That sentence became part of the family language. The children began asking, "Is this a cushion thing?" That is how a workbook becomes culture.

Their Next Generation Commitment

The Thompsons did not have a Level 5 asset yet, but they did have a Level 5 intention. They wanted their children to inherit skills, discipline, and eventually ownership. They wrote a commitment that fit their actual life:

We are building so our children know how to fix, save, decide, and own. We may not hand them everything, but we will not hand them nothing.

Their first next-generation action was not a trust. It was a family binder: birth certificates, insurance information, account list, emergency contacts, and the children's savings goals. Structure begins with order.

CLUES FOR THE READERS

- If your income is hourly, your plan must respect variable pay and real-life pressure.
- Small automatic transfers count. They build identity before they build large balances.
- Children's skills are part of the family's HUELOC.
- If you do not yet have Level 5 assets, you can still write Level 5 values

KEY TAKEAWAY

The Thompsons prove that Levels of Liquidity is not only for people with large portfolios. A cushion can begin with $25, a written rule, and a family meeting. The amount matters, but the commitment comes first.

RENEE

Entrepreneur

Cash flow, tax discipline, and legacy architecture

Fictional composite for teaching purposes. Not financial, legal, tax, or investment advice. Readers should adapt the clues to their own situation and consult qualified professionals where appropriate.

Case Study 5 — Renee: The Entrepreneur

Profile

Renee is 47 and owns a growing event production company. Some months are excellent. Some months are tight. She has learned how to sell, negotiate, hire, and solve problems at midnight. She is talented, but her finances have often followed the emotional rhythm of the business: feast, famine, catch up, repeat.

Renee came to the workbook after a profitable year that did not feel profitable. Revenue was high, but cash was scattered. She had upgraded equipment, leased a new vehicle, paid contractors late twice, and used personal accounts to cover business gaps. Her chair was not a lack of opportunity.

Her chair lacked separation and structure.

THE CHAIR PRESSURE

Her Quick Start sentence was blunt:

"Right now, money feels heavy because my business looks successful, but I do not always know which money belongs to the business, the tax bill, my household, or the future."

That sentence opened the door to the Tax Illusion section. Renee had been proud of deductions, but she had not always asked whether the spending built a cushion. She needed to stop confusing reduced taxable income with increased wealth.

Their Starting Cushion Map

Level	What Renee Had	Purpose She Assigned
Level 0 — HUELOC	Brand reputation, vendor relationships, event expertise, sales ability	Build team, systems, and intellectual property
Level 1 — Liquid	Business operating account and personal checking, sometimes mixed	Separate business operations from household spending
Level 2 — Reserve	$4,000 personal reserve; inconsistent business reserve	Build separate household and business emergency reserves
Level 3 — Self-Liquidating	Event planning templates and training ideas, not monetized	Create downloadable systems, paid workshops, licensing
Level 4 — Foundation	Retirement account underfunded, business equipment, insurance needs review	Long-term protection and owner independence
Level 5 — Next Generation	Business brand and client list	Build a sellable/transferable business, not just a job
Level 6 — Future Generation	Not yet	Future foundation or community training arm

WHAT RENEE LEARNED IN THE WORKBOOK

Renee's first lesson was that a business can be an asset or a demanding job, depending on structure. If the business cannot operate without constant personal rescue, it is not yet a strong cushion. If the business creates repeatable income, documented systems, and transferable value, it begins moving toward Level 5.

The Tax Illusion section challenged her. She remembered buying equipment in December because someone told her it would help with taxes. The equipment was useful, but the decision had not been part of a build plan. Going forward, she wrote a new question at the top of her office whiteboard: Does this purchase build a cushion or only reduce a tax bill?

The Private Family Office section also became practical. Renee did not need a billionaire's office. She needed a coordinated circle: CPA, attorney, banker, insurance expert, financial advisor, and eventually a project manager/bookkeeper who could help keep the pieces aligned.

Her 90-Day Build Plan

- **Level 1 habit:** fully separate business and personal accounts; pay herself on a schedule.
- **Level 2 goal:** build a $10,000 business reserve and a $10,000 personal reserve before major upgrades.
- **Tax discipline:** meet with CPA quarterly instead of only at tax time.
- **Level 3 build:** package her event checklist and vendor training into a paid digital toolkit.
- **Level 5 action:** document core business systems so the company has value beyond Renee's personal labor.

Her first seven-day action was administrative, not glamorous. She opened a separate tax savings account and created a rule that a percentage of every client payment would be routed there before she paid anything else. Then she scheduled a CPA meeting before the next busy season

Their "We Will Not Touch" Rule

Renee wrote:

"I will not use personal Level 2 money to cover business disorganization. If the business needs cash, I will review pricing, receivables, expenses, and reserves before pulling from household cushions."

She also wrote a business rule:

"I will not make year-end purchases only because they are deductible. Every purchase must have a business purpose and a cushion purpose."

Those rules gave her business a new kind of maturity. She was no longer reacting to cash flow. She was building a system.

Their Next Generation Commitment

Renee has one adult son who has watched her work hard for years. She does not know whether he will ever want to run the company, but she does know she wants the business to become transferable. That changed her Level 5 thinking. A business that only Renee understands dies with Renee's energy. A business with systems can outlive the founder.

Her commitment read:

"I am building a business that can teach, employ, transfer, or be sold. I am not only creating income. I am creating an asset with instructions."

Her Level 6 vision was a future foundation or training institute for young entrepreneurs in her city. She did not start there. She wrote it down as a direction, then returned to the 90-day work: clean accounts, clear reserves, documented systems.

CLUES FOR THE READERS

- If you own a business, separation is protection.
- A deduction is not the same as a cushion.
- If income is irregular, your rules must be written before the high month arrives.
- Level 3 may be hiding inside your process: templates, trainings, systems, licensing, or content.
- ·A business becomes Level 5 when it can outlive the founder's daily labor.

KEY TAKEAWAY

Renee did not need a bigger business first. She needed a cleaner one. The workbook helped her move from revenue to structure, from deductions to cushions, and from founder exhaustion to transferable value.

LIQUIDITY BASICS

What This Is All About

LIQUIDITY BASICS
WHAT THIS IS ALL ABOUT

The single most important idea in this entire workbook

Liquidity is not just a financial term. It is a decision.

Every asset you own exists for a purpose. Knowing that purpose — and honoring it — is the difference between building wealth that lasts one hundred years and spending your cushions the moment life gets uncomfortable.

What liquidity means

Liquidity describes how quickly an asset can be converted to cash. A checking account is fully liquid — today. A piece of land is not liquid — months. In the Levels of Liquidity system, liquidity is not just a description. It is a declaration of intent. When you assign a level to an asset, you are deciding what it is for — and what it is not for.

Change today to get to tomorrow

The gap between where you are and where you want your family to be in one hundred years is not closed by one dramatic decision. It is closed by thousands of small decisions made correctly — starting today.

Three questions to ask before every financial decision

1. Which level does this money belong to?
2. Am I moving a cushion up — or removing one?
3. Would I make this same decision in writing, with my name on it?

If you cannot answer all three, wait. The cushion is more important than the urgency.

GLOSSARY OF TERMS

The Levels of Liquidity framework introduces several original concepts. This glossary defines each one clearly so they can be referenced quickly during a workshop, masterclass, or personal review session.

Asset
Anything you own that holds or generates value. Assets are the cushions in the Levels of Liquidity framework.

Build Principle, The
The rule that every asset must be fed and grown continuously. A stronger asset provides stronger protection and stronger liquidation power when needed.

Cushion
The central metaphor of this framework. Every asset you build is a cushion placed on top of the chair — your starting point. The more cushions you stack, the less you feel the difficulty of the base.

Dual-Level Principle
The concept that a single asset can occupy more than one liquidity level based on your written declaration of intent. An asset's level is not fixed by type — it is fixed by purpose.

Human Equity Line of Credit (HUELOC)
The total value of your human capital — your skills, knowledge, discipline, relationships, and reputation — expressed as a financial asset that funds every level above it. Introduced in Build Your Human Equity Line of Credit by Steven E. LaBroi.

Level 0
Human capital. The foundational asset beneath all financial assets. The first investment a parent makes in a child, and the first investment any wealth builder makes in themselves.

Level 1 — Liquid
Cash, checking accounts, and debit — assets available for daily and monthly living expenses.

Level 2 — Reserve
Savings accounts, money market funds, and emergency reserves covering 3-6 months of expenses.

Level 3 – Self-Liquidating
Assets that generate income without being sold – royalties, intellectual property, dividends, and annuities. The income they produce is routed upward to build stronger levels.

Level 4a – Life Insurance
Whole life and indexed universal life policies functioning as a private family bank – funded continuously, borrowed against rather than sold, with a death benefit that transfers tax-free to the next generation.

Level 5 – Next Generation Assets
Land, commercial real estate, family business, and life insurance death benefits – assets committed to future generations, leveraged but never sold, with values that appreciate across a lifetime.

Level 6 – Future Generation Assets
Digital currency, cryptocurrency, global business interests, and emerging asset classes held inside permanent legal structures – trust foundations, 508(c)(1)(a) organizations, PMAs, and dynasty trusts – for a 100-year generational horizon.

Leverage Rule, The
The principle that debt against an appreciating asset is not a liability – it is a tool. Level 5 real estate is refinanced, not sold. The property pays the debt. The family inherits clean.

Liquidity
How quickly and easily an asset can be converted to cash. In this framework, liquidity is not just a description – it is a decision about purpose and intent.

Liquidity Level
The category assigned to an asset based on its purpose, holding period, and liquidation conditions. Levels range from 0 (human capital) to 6 (future generation structures).

Net Worth
Assets minus liabilities. The fundamental equation of wealth: Assets - Liabilities = Net Worth.

Private Family Office
A coordinated team of six professionals – Banker, Attorney, Insurance Expert, Financial Advisor, Tax Advisor, and Project Manager – who manage every dimension of a family's wealth infrastructure together.

Reinvestment Routing Rule
The principle is that income generated by self-liquidating assets (Level 3) is routed upward to build stronger levels rather than returned to consumption.

Self-Liquidating Asset
An asset that generates income without being sold. It liquidates itself on a schedule. The owner's job is to grow the asset and route the income strategically.

Tax Illusion, The
The mistake of confusing a tax deduction with wealth building. A deduction reduces what you owe — it does not build a cushion. Spending money to save on taxes without analyzing the total cost is one of the most common and expensive errors in wealth building.

508(c)(1)(a)
A faith-based non-profit organizational structure that operates with significant autonomy and tax protection, capable of holding and deploying assets for community and family mission across generations.

Dynasty Trust
A legal trust structure designed to hold and protect assets across multiple generations — in some states, indefinitely — shielding Level 5 and Level 6 assets from estate taxes and creditor claims.

Private Member Association (PMA)
A private contractual organization that operates outside many standard regulatory frameworks, offering

AFFIRMATIONS

The following affirmations are drawn from the author's published works—Build Your Human Equity Line of Credit and Financial Erudition of African Americans. They are included here as a daily practice for the wealth builder who understands that mindset is the foundation of every financial decision.

Touch 3 of 3 — The reinforcement

You have now completed every section of this workbook.

You have inventoried your assets, written your build plans, declared your liquidation conditions, and committed to your 100-year vision.

Now read the foundation one more time — with the eyes of someone who has built.

It will mean something different than it did the first time.

Affirmations for Building a HUMAN EQUITY LINE OF CREDIT LIFE

I believe in NO DEBT and true wealth

I believe in a stress-free lifestyle, paying limited taxes, and minimal interest

I believe in consuming as a real choice, not a compelled action

I believe in generational intelligence and moving information forward to my network and family

I believe in changing the paradigm of wealth building for my family and teaching others

I believe in creating great lives for future generations by creating new traditions and legacy building

I believe in creating financial tools for my income while I am living, and passing along those tools with wealth to the next three generations

— From Build Your Human Equity Line of Credit by Steven E. LaBroi

Notes

Use these pages to capture insights, commitments, and ideas that arise as you work through the framework — in this workbook, in the masterclass, or in conversations with your family and advisors.

Notes

Use these pages to capture insights, commitments, and ideas that arise as you work through the framework — in this workbook, in the masterclass, or in conversations with your family and advisors.

ABOUT THE AUTHOR

Steven E. LaBroi did not come to financial education through a university endowment or a Wall Street trading desk. He came through the same door most of his readers will recognize — the door of a family that worked hard, built what it could, and watched too much of it disappear between generations because no one had ever handed them a map. That absence of a map became his life's work.

He is the **Chief Strategist of LaBroi Insurance Group LLC**, a nationwide independent life insurance and retirement strategy firm he founded in 2015. Through LaBroi Insurance Group, Steven has spent over two decades helping families move from income dependence to asset ownership — from financial participation to financial control.

Steven is the **Executive Director of the nonprofit Millennial Banking Concept,** which equips young adults with financial literacy and wealth-building tools early in life. He is also the **Director of the Balance Life Health Wealth and Faith Institute**, a 508(c)(1)(a) ministry that assists individuals and families in balancing the foundational trilogy of human life: Health, Wealth, and Faith — creating a state of peace when achieving balance with life's demands.

A graduate of Morehouse College in Atlanta, Georgia, with a degree in Finance and Banking, Steven brings a disciplined, culturally grounded, and faith-centered approach to every framework he builds. His education gave him the language of finance. His life gave him the reason to teach it.

Steven is the author of the Amazon bestseller **Build Your Human Equity Line of Credit** — a work that challenges traditional financial thinking and introduces life insurance as a powerful, cash-flow-driven asset. He is also the co-author of **Financial Erudition of African Americans**, written alongside Dr. Anita R. Johnson — one of the most direct and culturally grounded financial literacy resources available to first-generation wealth-building families.

Beyond the page, Steven is an executive producer of the film Things Never Said, starring Omari Hardwick and Shanola Hampton, supporting the work of his childhood friend and acclaimed Hollywood writer and director Charles Murray. He is an active real estate investor and landlord whose experience with property ownership informs the practical, unsentimental advice in this workbook on leveraging real estate without ever selling it. He has lived the difference between liquidating an asset and leveraging one. He teaches from that difference, not from theory.

The Levels of Liquidity framework represents years of thinking about why wealth built in one generation so often fails to survive into the next. The answer LaBroi found was not a lack of effort or intelligence — it was a lack of intentional structure. People were building assets without purposes. Making liquidation decisions in moments of crisis that should have been made in moments of clarity. Confusing tax deductions for wealth building. Carrying no framework for thinking beyond their own lifetime.

Levels of Liquidity was built to solve all of that — in plain language, with fill-in pages, with real examples drawn from real life, and with a vision large enough to span one hundred years.

Steven E. LaBroi is a financial educator, author, entrepreneur, and builder in the truest sense of the word. He measures success not in what he has accumulated but in what he has transferred — to his family, to his community, and now, through this workbook, to every reader who is ready to stop starting over and start building something permanent.

Works by Steven E. LaBroi

Financial Erudition of African Americans — co-authored with Dr. Anita R. Johnson
Build Your Human Equity Line of Credit
Levels of Liquidity: The Net Worth Bible Workbook
Balance Life, Health, Wealth, and Faith Institute

CONNECT WITH THE AUTHOR

For press, speaking engagements, podcast, and article writing
📞 Office: 202-544-6226
📧 Email: slabroi@labroiinsurancegroup.com
🌐 Website: labroiinsurancegroup.com

Connect on Social Media
Facebook: Steven LaBroi
Instagram: @slabroi
LinkedIn: linkedin.com/in/Stevenlabroi

Schedule an Appointment
📅 Book a Consultation:
labroiinsurancegroup.com/book

Book Distribution
📖 Available through Amazon and IngramSpark for worldwide distribution.

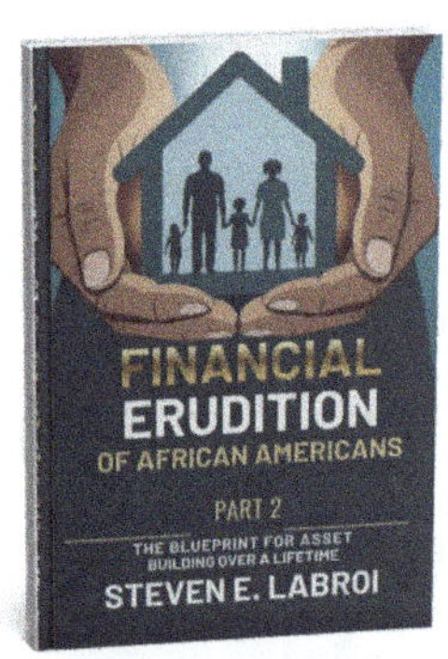

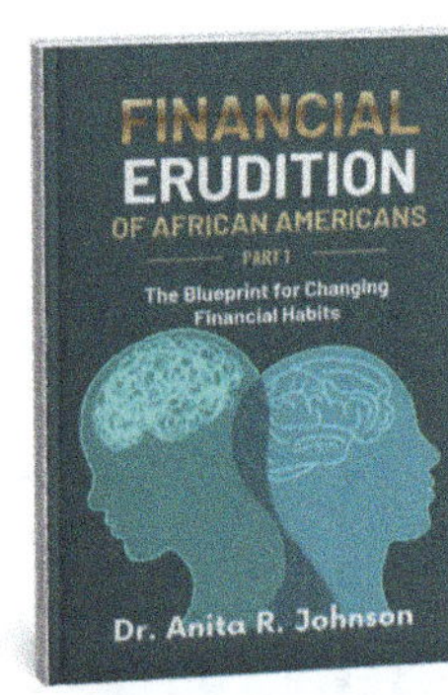

www.ingramcontent.com/pod-product-compliance
Lightning Source LLC
LaVergne TN
LVHW082349200926
848481LV00012B/3510

* 9 7 9 8 9 9 6 2 7 0 6 0 6 *